The following list contains names that I've collected over the past thirty years and have a personal connection with: either a direct encounter, encountered by friends/relatives and given to me, or gleaned from newspaper articles etc. Some of these names are included because there is something interesting, unusual or unique about them, perhaps the sound, spelling etc.   Some of them have a story connected to them, an interesting anecdote perhaps, or the name relates to an occupation or a situation that renders it interesting and therefore has been included.

The following legend has been included to explain the source. An asterisk * indicates newspaper documentation; UD indicates a name without documentation; S = Student, T = teacher, MS = the author, F = a friend, R = a relative, NYT= New York Times

* Ivy Mix, bartender at Leyenda, a bar in Cobble Hill, Brooklyn (NY T)

* David David David, (per the mother of a S I had (MS)

* Helen Fish, listing in obit right above Louis Freshwater (NYT)

* Douglas Duncan, arrested by two NYT city policemen while robbing a Duncan Donuts store. (Assoc Press Article 6-10-1998)

Dr. Smelsey, podiatrist–foot doctor, Oak Park, MI.(MS)

Dr. Ivan Doctor, Ophthalmologist (D. I. Doctor) Ferndale, MI (MS)

* Jean McClean, Sheraton Centre Hotel, Toronto, cleaning lady I met (MS)

* Kim Oatneal, makes cookies at Awrey Bakery, Livonia, MI (Observe&Eccentric paper 11-28-'99)

JoAnn Crabb, elementary school counselor at Our Lady Star of the Sea, Grosse Pointe, MI. (MS)

Robert Yenson, naval technician aboard ship sent to Iraq. He's known as ensign Yenson (MS)

* Boris Pistoff, basso profundo, performer with the La Gran Scena Opera Company.

* Capers Funnye, Michelle Obama's rabbi cousin. (NYT 3-11-2008)

* Chandraswamy, Indian Premier's Swami. (NYT 9-21-1995)

*Liborio Bellomo and Liborio Bellomo, cousins with the same name and nickname, Barney, and the same occupation: mobsters, described by F. B. I., as acting boss of the Genovese crime family. Which one? Exactly, the ones says, you got the wrong, Liborio. (Their fathers are brothers, and their mothers are sisters.) NYT

John John's John Bill, a bill in the Louisiana legislature requiring shopping malls to provide rest-room facilities, sponsored by Rep John Johns 111 (Readers Digest 2/'81)

* "Hong Kong is a colorful city, even—or perhaps especially—when it comes to English. A Penninsula Hotel publication cites the following: Chinese residents sometimes pick English names for themselves, i.e. Circumference Tse, Psych Poon, Motorbike Chan and Quasimodo Chang. One company had a women named Windy, a man named Sunny and a woman named Rainy, all working in the same department at the same time. When

translated from Cantonese the poetic names of some companies are grandlioquent. indeed: Lofty Virtue Printing.

Mary Ann Quinn, referee at the Wayne County Juvenile Court (Detroit, MI) reports on the following names she's run across. Detroit prostitutes name their kids after street on the east-side of Detroit hence: Baby Mt. Elliot, Baby Mack, Baby Chene, and Lonyo Exit Jones. Also Asshole, pronounced Azy O/Ley. (MS)

Marilyn Bagel, author of *The Bagel Bible*, a book on making bagels. (MS)

* Pork Chop Pugh, major league ball player, Cleveland and Detroit (F Howard Kaplan)

* Nicholas Economides, professor of economics at NY Univ.

* Chris Purgatori, therapist (Detroit Jewish News 6-12-'13)

Lee Musiker, Maureen McGovern's musical director, seen at DSO concert (MS 3-14-1993)

Daddy Barbee, fifth grade S at Bingham Farms El

Agent Justice, adult PO Oakland County, MI (R Nancy S.)

Kasha Munsky (friend of Jessica Trewern)

K̲nittel (K sound + nittel,) Student at CASA, Berkley, MI

A teacher named Hans has a brother named Lars (MS)

Mama Marenah, third grade black female S at Huron Academy (MS)

*Nico Charisse, dance teacher who married his student Tula Ellice Finklea, who became the dancer and actress Cyd Charisse

(NY T)

*Genghis Cohen, owner of an indoor shooting range: Machine Guns Vegas (NYT)

*Thilo Weissflog (letter to editor NYT)

*Michael Banks from Charter One Bank

David Wines, therapist specializing in addiction. (R Nancy S)

*Dr. William Lunn, heart transplant lung specialist with Dr. Debakey (NYT)

Joan Reddy, John Reddy's wife. Her maiden name is Mette (rhymes with Betty) her friends call her Joan Mette Reddy, her father is Teddy (MS)

*The Duke University Lacrosse Team rape case, officer investigating was named Himan. (NYT)

*Megan Smolenyah Smolenyak, a professtional genealogist. (NYT)

Zhelinrentice Clampitt running on primary ballot for Michigan State Legislature in district 17 (F Helene Skora)

*Michael House, residential real estate salesman, Real Estate One

*Judge Hubert Legal, actual French Judge. (NYT)

Uliviyya (Olivia) Musaboyoua, student

*Dusty Foggo, Top Spook (in 2004 picked by director of the CIA to be the No. 3 person in charge per Maureen Dowd (NYT)

K'nesha Starling (a student of mine when I taught in Detroit) she has six younger sisters: Tinesha, Latesha, Maneesha, Gruneisha, and Rachel (MS)

Sierra and Cierra, twin sisters, students of mine while teaching in Detroit (MS)

Elontra Hall, black male teacher in Farmington Hills (MS)

Morgan Morton (S at Farm Hills)

Norm Juchno (T in Farm Hills)

Cayla Dinwiddie (S at Hazel Park High School)

Charisma Alexander (S at Power Middle School, Farm Hills)

Hugo Stern (4th grade S at W. Bloomfield El)

Ti Che (Asian Student)

Amy Camaiani (UD a name randomly collected by me)

*Jesse James, a 37 year old bouncer at Queens, NY dance club.

*Preston Banks, TCF bank manager

*Nixzmary Brown, name in NYT of a young girl

Courteous Preston, S at Gill El Farm Hills (MS)

*Alan Lightman, an Astrophysicist—stars-light-space, heard on the radio.

Linda, Craig's wife, her maiden name was Stillwater, her mother's maiden name was Lightstone: she went from Lightstone to Stillwater

Sama Aso, student at Harrison High School, Farm Hills. In calling attendance I almost said what sounded like Sama A-hole before I checked myself.

*James F. English, chairman of the English department at University of Pennsylvania.

Dhanmite Slappey, star basketball player at Southfield Lathrup HS.(MS)

Beaula Plapinger & Ruth Shnittsky (Joe, a F went to school with them.)

Ivan & Ivon Shangi, brothers at Hazel Park HS

Forest Norris, S at Hazel Park Junior High

Xerxes Chinoy, an E. Indian S

*Dr. Kevin Eggan, involved in the cloning of human eggs.

Mrs. Weessies, music teacher Berkshire Middle School, Bhm, MI

Mary Monk, S at Berkshire Middle School, Bhm

Michael Putz and Simon Schuster (Ss at Derby M/S/Bhm)

Jacob June, S at Hazel Park Jr. High

*Smooch Reynolds, president and CEO of Repovich-Reynolds Group, Pasadena, CA

*Greg Craig, president Clinton's special council

*AmIgone, Funeral Home Operator, Buffalo, NY.   Dumfart,

name on tombstone.

*Theodore X. Barber, his son is X. Theodore Barber (obit NYT)

*J.J. Pickle, Texas Congressman—his daughter is Peggy Pickle. (obit NYT)

Nik Bibk, an elementary S I had at Longacre El., Farmington, MI. (MS)

*Captain Mariner, naval captain (MS heard on NPR 5-20-05)

At Harlan El, Bhm school, I had a girl student whose last name was Stein, her father is David, my son's name (May. '05)

*Cardinal Jaime Sin, one of Asia's most prominent religious leaders, NYT obit caption: Filipino Moral Compass Dies

*Sherri Hungerbuhler, restaurant manager. (NYT)

David David, S at Jardon school, Hazel Park;   Stepp Mayes, S at Pattengill El, Berkley.(MS)

Mrs. Teachworth, substitute teacher at Anderson Middle School, Berkley; <u>Jagger Huff</u>, S at Rogers El

Laura Kakarriqi, math T at Henderson H/S, Farm Hills

Alaina Mackool, Erin McClue, two S in same class Berkley school(Dec 2004)

*Bernard de Wattewille, established a breeding center for St. Bernard dogs.(Geneva)

*Lang Lang, famous piano player

*Jonathan Fairoaks, California based arborist and tree-house designer.(June '05)

January 20, 2005 – I substituted for Mrs. Kuhl in the a.m and Mrs. Doll in the p.m.

Miss Reid, library T at Angel El, Berkley

C. F. Flowers, landscaper specializing in flower gardening.

*Brick Mason, production aide on the movie *The Village*. M. Night Shamalan, director.

*Asaad Witwit, Iraqui Factory Owner (9-13-04)

*Adam Vonkerversdon, Canadian Kayak Olympic champion

*Captain Kevin Badger, US military commander leading an assault in Iraq.

 Seven, first name of a child, last name? (per Catholic School Counselors I met.)

*Dr. Adaora A. Adimora, infectious disease physician

*Geoff Menu, a waiter at Fred's Uptown Tavern in Vancouver, BC

Collusion To The Confusion, rock group name.

Lovely Legs; Governor Cherry; Virginia Mary Broom (names provided by Sue, a former gas co employee. She actually spoke to the these people. I met Sue at American Housing Survey Census Training.

Tony Williams Sr.; Tony Williams Jr.; Toni Williams, father, son, daughter all in same family (per Dalila, S at St. Scholastica.)

Ben Gay and Chuck Wagon (T at St. Scholastica said her sister who worked for Vic Tanney actually signed these two men up for memberships. They were friends and she saw their driver's licenses.(10/12/1994)

*Craig Stock, personal finance columnist for the Philadelphia Inquirer.

*Dr. Snifendorfer, Cleveland Clinic cardiologist (too bad not an Eye Ear and Nose doctor)

Chris Burkeybigle, S at Norup Jr. High. O'Shetisi Okagbare, a black female S in the school.

*Bonnie Bucharoo, assn't director school of criminal justice at MSU (F Howard Kaplan)

*Shakeima Cabbagestalk (missing person poster)

Mr. Piggette T at Oakland Univ. (4-4-00)   Mr. Hogg, T at Oakland Comm College.

Barbie Dahl (per Kevin & Debbie, R) a S they knew at MSU.

*Adrianne Bloom- gardener, spokes person for Victory Garden in Capetown S. Africa.(2-10-97)

Patricia Christmas, female clerk at Michaels Arts & Crafts.

*God Shammgod, former Providence College point guard signed by the Washington Wizards.

*Robert Bookman, a top Hollywood literary agent.

*Carol Leigh, prostitute quoted in paper.

*Jeff Undercoffer, Secret Service agent assigned to the White House

Dr. Aiken (ache in) dentist that Marty, a friend went to.

*Seaborne Weathers of Dallas, caught in a blizzard that killed eight climbers.

*Word Baker, his daughter is Barbara Page. (Obit NYT)

*Eagle Eye Cherry, daughter of jazz artist Don Cherry

Fyvush Finkel, famous Yiddish actor

Sandy Sweetapple, sub T at Hazel park Special Ed Class

K. Dickensheets, vocal music T.

*Steve Wynn, owner of several hotels in Las Vegas

*Wendy Superfisky, (per newspaper article)

*Bam Morris, name of pro football player, he fits in with Bo, Bubba, Bump, and Bim, also sports figures.

Kat Sipple, art T.

*Peter Achoo, eye specialist in Lake Orion (he should have been a nose specialist)

Tonya Potter, ceramics S, Mr Daenzer, Walled Lake Central (11-9-91)

Murpherey Fitten, works at 12 & Evergreen Amoco gas station, Southfield, MI

Eric Cockream, S at Hazel Park High

Thankamamie Krishnon, doctor of a S I met at Henry Ford

It is apparently a common practice in Brazil to name children all beginning with the same or similar letters/sounds, hence: Emerson, Ilmerson, Anderson, three brothers in same family, last name? (Enelse, Brazilian T at St. Scholastica)

Xerxes(pronounced Cerseas) Preston, a S at St. Scholastica

*James Graves, Hinds County Circuit Judge, presided over a case involving a funeral home.

*Enid Fanfair, real estate Agent

*Mail sent to me(Myron Stein) addressed to: Maron Spein

Dr. Tingaling, orthodontist (Cindy, T at St. Scholastica 11-3-1994)

Tristan Tzara (Dadist artist formerly named Sam Rozenstock (R Chuck T.)

Rakestraw Ashberry, a name that seems to run in families (R Chuck T.)

Elimelach Goldberg; Paysach Krohn, Rabbi's names.

Kcathey, pronounced Cathy, clerk I met at Kinkos.(MS)

*Queen King, home owner near Detroit City Airport (Det Free Press)

*"The strength and the consistency of the research is enough that we can infer that physical inactivity causes heart disease," says John R. Livengood, M.D., chief of cardiovascular health at the Centers for Disease Control and Prevention in Atlanta.

Wonderful Terrific Montis (parents had several (12?) girls and when a boy came around they thought it was....

*Anna Smashnova, tennis pro, who whacked a ball in a fury toward an opponent but hit a bystander.

Eunice Wickersham, handweaving artist at Ann Arbor Art Fair (7-18-97)

*"A particularly sad situation, to me, is the plight of the only child in an alcoholic family. My experience with these children, confirmed by the finding of the Booz-Allen Report...."

Jay Crystal, watch maker (Mike Ross.)

*Absolutely Nobody, who legally changed his name from David Powers after his unsuccessful 1992 bid for Oregon lieutenant governor.(obit NYT)

*Research on Needle Hygiene and Needle Exchange Programs n Maryland. Contact Dr. Richard Needle.

Truly Boring, as seen on T.V. news, she was interviewed, 10-20-1994

Geebie Early (Gee as in gee whiz) a S at Hazel Park High

Theodora Bear goes as Teddy Bear (UD)

Sandy Shore (Linda, a F)

Linda, a friend has a friend who goes to a proctologist named Dr. Duffy.

*Candace A. Champagne, a lecturer, topic, Club Drugs Are No Party.

Mr. Ogle of Lakeside Mobile, White Lake, MI.

* Debra Cantor, Rabbi, therefor, properly Rabbi Cantor.

* Sir Vincent Wigglesworth, insect expert(Obit 3-14-1994) per F Ron Barnett

Dr. Hertz, a dentist (Ray & Roz, friend of the Mintz's, he's their dentist)

Paris Milan, flight rewards program clerk with Chase Manhattan Bank, Visa card, I spoke to on 1-5-2000) regarding their travel miles program.

Mary Misfud, S at Frost Middle School, Livonia, MI

Spookie Gouhl, S born on Halloween per F Tom Hildebrandt.

* Dr. Henry Bone, a bone specialist at Henry Ford Hospital per F Annette Rose

Ruthie Titinfish, and Franklin Delano Rosenblatt (F Marsha Barnett)

Stromeg Johnson (mother couldn't spell strong man)

Gornish Gelt (no money in Yiddish) per F Linda Shewach

* Wallingford Rewigger, music instructor at Conway Military school, Ithaca, NY., he taught Les Brown(1-6-2001)

*Atswhatimtallknabout, horses name, who because of an injury did not run in the Belmont Stakes.

Dr. Sain, psychiatrist at Help Source, David Stein's employer, a foster care agency.

Rear Admiral Craig Quigley, a pentagon spokesman.

Dr. Thabet Thabet, hi ranking Palestinian Health official assimilated into Israel.

Frank Church, pastor of church in Washington, D.C.

Jeff John, member of the Boyscouts.

*Beauty Piccirilli, parent of S at Our Lady of Refuge, (MS

Mrs. DeJardin (garden in French) liked working on her garden, my daughter worked for her. (MS)

Margaret Trout Pomeroy seen by MS on plaque in Hospice House, Pomeroy is the name of a fish store in W. Bloomfield, MI.

Faina Shub, I met her father at her Bat Mitsvah at Beth Shalom 12-23-1998

George Wren, new manager of the Baltimore Orioles (10-1998)

Jimmy Fish, who became a navy frogman (neighbor of a friend, Linda)

J. Michael Sprott (sprout?) Director of Cooperative Extension Service, Ohio State Univ. they give horticultural advice 5-14-1998

John Rhodes, public service spokesman for the Wayne County Road Commission reporting on the condition of the roads.(MS)

Mr. Greener, assistant manager of the green house at English Gardens (F Linda 12-7-1997)

Tom Cash, senior VP of financial services American Express.

* Armond Lamb, meat manager at Farmer Jack supermarket

* Lopez Betancourt, law professor

* Chamique Holdsclaw, basketball player Tennessee Univ. (Fined for holding?)

* Xavjeir Goodfaith, 15 year old from Oakland, CA, keeping faith at the eternal flame for JFK.

* Bicentual Long, slashed by an outraged lover while engaged in a consensual affair.

Sarah Serra, a relative of Chris Migliori, fellow T at St. Scholastica (MS)

Cutie Francis, the mistress of a Caribbean doctor (NYT MS)

* Julius R. Lunsford, retired from Coca-Cola and the took a job with Browne Beveridge (obit NYT 9-30-1999)

* Hugh Fish, who made the Thames so clean the salmon came back. (obit, 1999)

* Bubba Baker, Detroit Lions football player.

* Sir Valiant Brown, George Washington freshman point guard.

Clay Woody, S at Mr. Deluca's art class Walled Lake Central. (MS)

Per-olaf Loof, president of Sensormatic Electronics (per NYT article 7-8-2001 Pg 14.)

Nita Virgin, parent of S at Our Lady of Refuge (MS)

Sparrow, first name of a parent at St. Patrick's School, White Lake, MI per Linda Cederberg a T. 8-29-2001

* Sandra Sampson, customer service rep at blue cross (our good friend is Sandra Samson)

Myles Drive (per Linda, a customer at her beauty shop, she comes a long way?)

* James Shuttleworth, he paid millions of dollars to be the second

private citizen to be a passenger in a rocket launched recently (4-28-2002)

Billy Drummond, jazz drummer (heard by MS on Martin Van Dyke jazz show on NPR.)

Clown Davis, an assistant to Dr. Patch Adams—a movie based on his life—worked as a clown entertaining kids then officially changed her name

Zoe Bowie, David Bowie's daughter.

*Debbie Dingell, wife of U.S. Rep John Dingell.(August 2002)

* An innocent tippee, term used to describe someone who obtained inside information but did not regard it as such when she sold shares (per NYT) 8-6-2002

* Lawrence Beard, heavily bearded man in paper who admitted to a crime.

* Smush Parker, Cleveland basketball player (F H. Kaplan 12-24-2002)

* General John P. Jumper, Air Force General

* Tom Finkelpearl, Queens, NY Museum Director

* Nefertiti Thompson, sales rep at Sherry Washington gallery, Detroit.

* Shusha Guppy, author of A Panoramic View of a Literary Age by the Grandes Dames of European letters per (NYT obit)

Kellie G. Kelley, food writer, Cooking Light Magazine.

Rebecca Pate, food writer Cooking Light Magazine (March/April 1994)

June Flora, Phd at Stanford Univ. on Nutrition Action Magazine, advisory board.

Spooky Gouhl, Candy Apple, Penny Nichols. (Tom, a friend went to school with them) Nov. 2003

* Debra Grassgreen (per MS)

Buford Blunt, Brigadeer General during Iraq war.(MS)

Jose Jose, a S who wrote a letter to the president (NPR radio 12-2002)

Robert Vale or Veil, spokesman for the attorney general's office of Florida, commenting on a suit brought by a Muslim woman who claimed she was preventing form practicing her religion when she was refused to have had her drivers license photo with her face covered. (MS heard it on the radio. 7-30-2002)

Pang Hang, student at Hazel Park High School (MS)

Joan Rosen, cousin Howard's mother -in-law. She was born Joan Rose, married Herbert Rosen becoming Joan Rosen. He died and she married Joe Rose, so once again becoming Joan Rose. (obtained during Howard & Michelle's wedding 12-15-2002)

Dr. Emmy Gut, psychoanalyst (MS)

Dr. Pathwater, urologist; Dr. Bones, Orthopedic Surgeon; Dr. Fear, dentist, (per Linda, a friend. 10-2-2002)

Following names provided by St. Patrick teachers I worked with: Judy, 3rd grade T, once had a S named Crystal Glass; Michelle, 6th grade T, her sister teaches on an Indian reservation and had a family whose last name was, Smells Like A Skunk, they had regular first names, ie Sam etc.; Nancy, 5th grade T, her neighbor attended school in the east, Pennsylvana, and had a teacher named Ima Pigg.

Linda, a friend, her mother's proctologist is Dr. Duffy.(9-29-2001)

Putname Purchase, doctor who delivered Mrs. Gorny's, Our Lady of Refuge, 3rd grade teacher, 3rd child.

Archie Lopp, albino S with white hair and glasses, 3rd grade, S at Our Lady of Refuge

Santiago Martinez aka Ago 2nd grade S per Kim Levasseur, 2nd grade T at Our Lady of Refuge (he always wore very nice cologne.)

Dr. Ovary, not a gynecologist, unfortunately. (MS)

* Actual Rodeo Names: Steve Dollarhide, Buster Record Jr., Blue Stone, Spud Duvall, Rope Myers.

Winifred Crackle, per F Helene a friend, a S she knew. (4-23-2001)

Mickey Bass, jazz musician, plays string bass (per Ed Love jazz program WDET 101.9) 3-16-2001

Dana Fudge, from Licking, Missouri (works with our son David, at Help Source-- 2-26-2001)

* John Blandford he is survived by his wife Betty Blakely Blandford (obit NYT)

Rex Lux, S of Kendall, Our Lady of Refuge T, memorable because he had perfect handwriting, much better than the teachers.

Mark Cheese, pastry chef at Courtyard Cafe, Windsor Arms

Hotel, Toronto, CA.(MS 2-19-2001)

Cynthia Wine, restaurant critic of Toronto Globe (MS 2-19-2001)

Mary Philpott, potter, her bowls are on display at Gardner Museum of Ceramic art.(MS 2-19-2001)

* Steve Salmon, manager at Morton's, a steak restaurant.

* Biff Liff, agent with Willliam Morris talent agent (NYT 12-1-2000)

Chandeu Lear, Lear Jet family, per Marlena, secretary at Southfield Center for the Arts.7-12-1002

Chief Crook, top cop in Montgomery County Alabama, (NYT columnist Maureen Dowd 10-16-2002)

Joan Surnamer (need I explain?) (NYT 11-17-2003)

Mindy Fullilove, professor of Clinical psychiatry and public health at Columbia University (NYT magazine 10-12-2003)

* Ella Bully Cummings, Detroit Police chief, 11-22-2003

Saudi, Arabia and Jihad Porter, S of cousin Debbie; she's also aware of another S named Almighty God (last name unknown); 12-21-2003

* Unusual southeast Michigan street names: Butwell, Livonia; Going, Pontiac; Nummer, Warren; Quirk Road, Van Buren Township.

* Horst Horst, Vogue magazine fashion photographer

*Ruth Greenhouse, director of education at the Desert Botanical Garden, Phoenix, AZ

Usain Bolt, Jamaican runner considered to be the world's fastest human being (I saw him win the 100 and 200 meters men's sprint at the 2008 Beijing summer Olympics, breaking world records both times, as he literally bolted out from the rest of the runners. (MS)

Lynda Sing, an ensemble singer/dancer in *The Music Man*, seen at Stratford Shakespearean Festival, Ontario, Canada (August 2008)

Lyric Cheeks, 2nd grade S in Miss Purdue's class at Malcolm X Academy (MS)

* George W. George, Broadway producer (obit NYT)

Gregory McNamee, lecturer at Casa Grande Ruins National Park, 1 hour from Tucson, AZ. His lecture was on the history of Arizona Place names. (2-24-2008) MS

* Photo of Lindsay Pears being offered fruit. (NYT 9-5-2007)

* African man, Ademu, he had three wives and 20 children, he called the children Hey You and This One (per article in April 2008 issue of National Geographic.)

Vicki Payne, woman glass blower/artist (per our daughter, Tobey)

* Frank Saysno, NPR host on a discussion about sex education.(R Tobey 2008)

* Carol Schmekel, director of surgical services, Beaumont Hospital Troy.

House Peters Jr., (NYT obit)

Cherrard Cohen, a very dark skinned African American boy at Berkshire M/S, c'mon is he really Jewish? (MS 9-25-2008)

* Tom Carpenter, an electrician (NYT business section 10-31-

2008)

Parker Pickell, a S at Quarton El school, Bhm, MI (MS 10-28-2008) I also ran into him at Derby M/S.

* Martin Flumenbaum, NY city attorney.

Nathan Redwine, a Middle School S I met (MS)

* Dr. Mazoltuv Borukhova (in Yiddish Mazoltuv is congratulations,) but this doctor has nothing to celebrate as she was charged with murder.(NYT 2-5-2009)

Hana Ljuljdjuraj, Albanian M/S S I met in Farmington (MS)

Mrs. File, receptionist at Berkshire M/S, Bhm, MI (MS)

* Christopher Bird, bird expert at the University of Cambridge, London

Oululu Bien, and Amazin ? Ss, cousin Debbie has had in class. (11-10-2001)

Terrell Louis and Louis Terrell, Ss in a class cousin Debbie knows the T, it drove her crazy.

Marmaduke Pickthall (MS UD)

Fair Hooker, former Cleveland Browns receiver

* Ed Thigpen, jazz drummer (obit)

Van Lingle Mungo, Brooklyn Dodgers pitcher of the 1930's. He led the National League in strike outs with 238 in 1936. He won 120 games and lost 115 with the Dodgers & Giants.

The Secret Man, Bob Woodward's book about the disclosure of the identity of "Deep Throat". He was Mark Felt, second in charge of the FBI at that time. The irony Woodward reveals is that he lived on Redford Place in Santa Rosa, CA., Dustin Hoffman along with Robert Redford starred in the movie *"All The Presidents Men,"* about the Watergate Scandal (7-31-2005)

Names gleaned from *Freakonomics*, the book by Steven Levitt and Stephen Dubner: See Chapter 6' Pg 79. A NY city father named Robert Lane who named his sons Winner Lane and Loser Lane. Winner did well; Loser has a long police record.

A teenage boy named Amcher, named after the first thing his parents saw upon reaching the **A**lbany **M**edical **C**enter **H**ospital **E**mergency **R**oom; Girl named Temptress, charged with "ungovernable behavior" which included bringing men home while her mother was at work.

A young couple named Tatalie Jeremyenko and Dalton Conley renamed their four-year old son, YoXing Heyno Augustus Eisner Alexander Weiser Knuckles Jeremi Jenko Conley.

A NY City cab driver named Michael Goldberg was shot in early 2004—it was reported that he was in fact an Indian born Sikh, who thought it advantageous to take on a Jewish name upon immigrating to New York.

Issur Danielovitch became Kirk Douglas; William Morris TalentAgency, namesake is Zelman Moses; A lady called into a radio show to say that she was upset with the name just given her baby niece. It was pronounced Shuh-teed but spelled Shithead.

And then there is Orangejello and Lemonjello, pronounced A-ron-zhello and Le-mon- Zhello. (S of a teacher friend of our friend, Varda)

St. Mychael Success, 8th grade S at East Middle School, Farm Hills (MS 4-14-2005)

Ayvin (Ivan) Slewoa, Chaldean S at East M/S (MS)

Happy Howes, S at Anderson M/S (MS)

* Filler – Quick, the marriage of.

Chidi Chidi, from Africa and father of Lynn Chidi a S at St. Scholastica. Had a long last name so changed last name to same as first name.

Faik Fahshew, a S of Inelsie DeRamo T at St. Scholastica. (MS 12-9-1995)

*Mike Deja, WJR-AM deejay.

Erin Rubenstein, a male Berkley High School S I met who explained his interesting but unusual name: His mother is Irish and his father, Jewish. (okay) He further told me that he has a girl friend named Chris Clark and that his sister has a boy friend named Kris Clark. (per MS 5-14-1993). I told this story to cousins Irene and Gary, Gary indicated that he worked with someone named Chris Clark.

Simon Simon, our daugher, Tobey knows this boys sister (5-10-1993)

Pang Chang, a Laotion girl in Roger Snell's class at Hazel Park High; her name is Pang Na Change, Na, means rain, Chang means flower, hence rain flour (6-11-1993)

Herta Feely, (MS UD)

Pamela Palms, art director Oakland Life Magazine (MS, 5-26-1993)

Wolfgang Puck, famous chef

Donal Dinwiddie, (per St. Anne craft book, editor of crafts & science articles (MS)

Monica Pighee, group sales dept Gem Theater (MS)

Winnie Wong, lawyer in Toronto's Chinatown, hopefully she winnies all her cases (MS 8/'93)

Crisby Workman, an African American male interviewed on T.V. (MS)

Tunch Ilkin, pro football player with Pittsburg Steelers, also on same team Bubby Brister (MS)

Bill Wisswell, seen on billboard on I-94, running for political office.(MS)

Ernie Jew, Jane Pipik (MS UD)

Merry Meldrum, S I had, (MS)

Ervin Kitchenmaster, owner of B's Blazing Speed, Hazel Park Racehorse, he didn't win.(MS 5-21-'93)

Brooksley Born, The nations first female Attorney General, appointed by Bill Clinton, Dec. '92

Phyllills Neufelt, fibers artist per The Family Workshop Vol 5, Pg 552 Plenary Publishers.

* William T. End, appointed CEO of Lands' End Inc.(1-30-'93)

Turley Mings, Economics text book author (MS)

Olden Polynice, Detroit Pistons player (MS 11/'92)

Launch Faircloth, southern politician. (11-3-'92)

Sara Zara, 3rd grade S, St. Anne Catholic School (MS)

Rosa Ooink, S at Hazel Park or Walled Lake Central, I subbed at both (MS)

Metropolitan Theodosius, head of Greek Orthodox church in America.

Rosebud Yellow, Robe Frantz, great grandchildren of chief Sitting Bull (MS)

* Clinton Gore, Traverse City, MI, dentist. He supported George Bush. (Neal Rubin Col. Det Free Press 11-4-1992)

I was working at Metro Beach, a man came to check in at tennis counter, he gave his name as Mike Monday, the man standing right behind him was Simms Friday. Mike Monday was in a bar recently, he said, and heard paged a customer, Mike Sunday. (MS this story occurred on 7-26-1992, day of the week?)

Wesley Green gardener, on T.V. show Victory Garden (MS)

Jackie Yackey, camper at Black River Riding Camp (per Linda a friend)

Dusty Rhodes, Southfield, MI policeman (MS)

Tabbitha Catt, a friend of Katy Mansell's

* Milan Panic, former minister of Yugoslalvia and founder of ICN Pharmaceuticals.

Fred Saintmary, Wanda Goodnough both patrons at Metro Beach (MS)

Olds Retirement Home, Grand Rapids, MI (MS)

C.C. VanLoan, president of First Security Bank, Ionia MI (MS 3-15-1987)

Mrs. Foster, Grand Rapids Michigan Association of Foster Parents, I met her (MS 2/'87)

Len Kracker, photographer (MS)

Greg/Craig Isakow, Jewish S at Birney M/S per Tobey (good thing he's Jewish otherwise he woulda been Isapig.)

Furney Revels, father is Gurney Revels, Cherokee Indians.(MS) anymore sibs?

* Opal Fleckenstein, artist of batik titled 'Half of a Full Moon" which consists of many flecks of color (American Crafts Council)

Belle Pepper, name seen in Detroit Jewish News (Linda S, 3-19-1993).

Malice Green, who was murdered with malice by a convicted Detroit Police Officer (11-14-1992)

Tasso Teftsis, owner of Greek Pastry Shop, Astoria, Detroit, MI.

Wimp Sanderson, basketball coach, Univ. of Alabama (5/'92)

Robin Parrott, fellow worker at Metro Beach, (MS 8/'91)

Nasar Nasar Nasar, grandfather of Jason Nasar, a S of mine (MS)

Jim Koger, Kroger striking worker (MS)

Lane Closure, traffic reporter, 104.3 radio, (Linda S)

Buddy Dikman, per 20/20 TV show on homosexuals. (MS)

* Bong Bong, son of Ferdinand and Imelda Marcos.

Julia Nevels Navel, involved in lawsuit. on TV 2-17-1992

Moella Hesselgrace (UD MS)

General P X Campbell (UD MS)

* Mr. Reagan Carter, who got much flack during election time but none from the business one door down from his: the Nixon Ford Motor Co. (Beaumont, Tex.-UPI story)

Billy Bupp (T Halycyon Kramer UD)

Merry Noel Meldrum, born two days after x-mas. S in Mrs. Qualkenbush class, Churdhill High School Livonia.(5-21-'93)

Tunga Constantennia (MS UD)

Sandy Heyer (pronounced hire) Head of Wayne Co. Personnel Office, Detroit, MI. (MS)

Skip Skoolnick, TV producer (MS UD)

Famous Coachman, record store operator, east side of Detroit, MI (MS)

Yer Her, Laotian S at Pontiac Adult Ed (MS)

Palombo Weingarten, Capers Jones (MS UD)

* Hippocrates Apostle, one of the foremost English language translators of Aristotle (obit)

Blimee Youngworth (MS UD)

*Ruth Kluth, finalist in cooking competition.

* "Detroit funeral director O'Neil Swanson helped deliver a baby in the parking lot of his east side funeral home. The mother, Davis, 16, in turn named the baby Swanmika Laneil after Swanson." (Detroit Free Press)

* Browne Greene, attorney

"A tail cone from a commercial jetliner dropped out of the sky onto Skye Drive in Farmington Hills, MI." (Detroit Free Press 4-2-'90)

Sandy Sweetapple, S teacher, Mrs. Zebawa special ed class, Roosevelt Elem., Hazel Park (MS)

Oleaner Miller, friend of the Mintz's

Moshe(Moosay) Kue, Asian S at Webb M/S, Hazel Park (MS) also Monther Matti, another S.

Angel Evangelist, S at Webb Jr. Hi, Hazel Park (MS)

Dallas West, custodian at Hazel Park H/S (MS)

Chopimup & Burnham, business at 12 Oaks Mall, Novi, MI. (MS UD)

Scott Knott, S at Hazel Park High (MS)

Jenny McKinney, S (MS)

Apple Wick, 6th grade S at Edison School, Hazel Park, MI (MS)

Jim Collias, winner of Victory Garden contest (1990) from Harper Woods, MI. (MS)

Hummie Mann, created the music for the movie *The Year of the Comet.* (MS 7-3-93)

* Kadesha, Nikeisha, Allisha, Lakisha, Mikesha, Latisha, Felicia, Takisha, 8Th grade S graduating Birney M/S, Southfield, MI, June 15, 1983

Demetrios "Jimmy" Papatriantafyllou and Tony Hadjisofroniou, well known Greek restaurant owners Detroit, MI. (Detroit Jewish News 9-24-2015)

* Your name is not wholly your own as much as you may think it is: see article, included with documented material by Sydney Harris, Detroit Free Press, 7/21/'79. also see article also by Sydney Harris dated 8/7/'74)

Leo Van Munching Jr., his father Leo van Munching preferred the lower case v, his son the upper case V. (obit NYT 2-16-'16)

Former World Heavyweight boxing champion, George Foreman, has five sons all named after him: George Jr, George 111, George IV, George V, George VI, he also has daughters named Georgetta and Freda George, his other three daughters are not named after him(10 kids in total).   He says, "If you're going to get hit as many times as I've been by Mohammed Ali, Joe Frazier, Ken Norton, Evander Holyfield, you're not going to remember many names." His wife concurs.

* "In southern Africa, a child's name is chosen to convey a specific meaning, and not, as is common in the West, the latest fashion." Some examples are:

    "Godknows Nare, a Zimbabwean videographer, the name given to him at age one when his parents feared   that he would die."

    "Have-a-Look Dube, is a well-known Zimbabwean soccer player."

    "A Bulawayo truck driver is named Smile, and true to form, he is never without a broad smile on his face."

    "If a Sotho-speaking girl becomes pregnant before marriage, her unhappy parents may name the baby Question or Answer –an answer to the question of why their daughter was behaving so strangely before the pregnancy became known"

(NYT International, Monday, October 1, 2007)

* Benjamin Millepied, A good looking French young man, the rage, a hot ballet dancer & choreographer married to the actress Natalie Portman, who was nominated for best actress for her role in Black Swan. His name in French means thousand footed. (NYT 2-3-'11)

* Dr. Sundeep Khosla,, a Mayo Clinic endocrinologist and president of The American Society for Bone and Mineral Research who applauded a report recommending the benefits of the body producing vitamin D after being out in the sun and storing it in their bodies.

Howard Sweet whose next door neighbor was Howard Sour, (per Dr. Larry Sweet, Village Player member who told me this, his father was Howard. (MS)

Marina Aarts, a specialist in 17th century art (from the book "The Forgers Spell," by Edward Dolnick pg 231, 4-29-'11)

Charles Gardner, driver of a Jacobson's Flower Co., truck (Nancy S. 3-24-'11)

* Judith Peixotto Sulzberger, daughter of Arthur and Iphigene Ochs Sulzberger (obit NYT 2-23-'11)

* Terry Drinkwine, Nancy S. new boyfriend. (Nov. 2010 Oakland Press)

Jinks Fires, horse trainer of Archarcharch. Jinks, at age seventy made his Derby debut. (Why did it take so long? You guessed it)

Sam Chwat, dialect tutor to the stars. (NYT obit)

George Georges, Tom Thomas, Nick Nicholas (per Jason,

Jannette S. boy friend who knows these guys (10-24-'12)

* Phyllis Cleveland, city councilwoman who represents—you guessed it.(MS)

Rabbi Avraham Yitzhak Hacohen Kook, Israel chief rabbi. (NYT obit 7-19-'12)

* Gu-Wonder Whitfield, uninsured who was able to get a long-delayed physical exam thanks to the health care ruling by the U. S. Supreme Court (Detroit Free Press)

* Boris Worm, lead author of a 2006 paper advocating the eating of fish.(NYT Op-Ed 4-15-'11)

* Harley Rider, former sheriff's deputy in Washtenaw County, Mi (yes, he does ride motorcycles but never owned a Harley Davidson motorcycle.)

* Valter Longo, director of the University of Southern California's Longevity Institute. (Time Mag. 2-22-'16)

Jimmer Fredette, the No. 10 draft pick in 2011, about to sign with the Knicks of the NBA. (NYT 2-22-'16)

On a road trip, stop for a bite to eat at: Two Eggs, Fla.; Toast, N.C.; Sandwich, Mass.; Burnt Corn, Ala.; Hot Coffee, Miss.; Tea, S.D.; Cookietown, Okla.; Popcorn Ind.; Chicken, Alaska; Turkey, Texas; Pie Town, N. M. (home of the two eateries: Good Pie Cafe and Pie-O-Never)

* "A 33-year-old British man legally changed his name to Bacon Double Cheeseburger. 'it was the culmination of...too many drinks in the pub,'" he said. (Time magazine, 3-7-2016)

Takee Outee, Chinese carryout restaurant, Utica, MI. (MS)

In conclusion I'd like to share a name story:

A friend, Marty, an administrative law judge with the State of Michigan had a case with a mother whose child had a very unusual name, Ezcarmartinez Zorro Jackson. Marty asked how the woman came up with this name and she replied that it had just came to her, but admitted that she was under the influence of medication at the time. Marty speculated as to how she came up with the name: When she was being wheeled into the delivery room on a gurney an attendant cautioned a reckless co-worker, "easy with the car Martinez." I added that it was a good thing that the didn't have the name come to her as she was being given an anesthetic or we'd have—you guessed it: Ezanetheezee.

I hope you have enjoyed this list as much as I have had putting it together. If you have a name that you would like to see added to this list, and are willing to share, feel free to contact me and I will gladly add it to the collection.

Sincerely,

Myron S. Stein, author

Printed in Great Britain
by Amazon

44324468R00020